W9-CMF-672

The Pebble® First Guide to

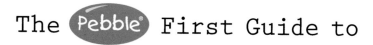

Spiders

by Megan Cooley Peterson

Consulting Editor: Gail Saunders-Smith, PhD

Consultant:
Gary A. Dunn, M.S.
Director of Education
Young Entomologists' Society Inc.
Minibeast Zooseum and Education Center

Consultant:
Laura Jesse
Iowa State University
Plant and Insect Diagnostic Clinic
Ames, Iowa

Capstone
press®
Mankato, Minnesota

Pebble Books are published by Capstone Press,
151 Good Counsel Drive, P.O. Box 669, Mankato, Minnesota 56002.
www.capstonepress.com

1 2 3 4 5 6 13 12 11 10 09 08

Library of Congress Cataloging-in-Publication Data
Peterson, Megan Cooley.
 The Pebble first guide to spiders / by Megan Cooley Peterson.
 p. cm. — (Pebble books. Pebble first guides)
 Includes bibliographical references.
 ISBN-13: 978-1-4296-1712-3 (hardcover)
 ISBN-10: 1-4296-1712-8 (hardcover)
 ISBN-13: 978-1-4296-2806-8 (softcover pbk.)
 ISBN-10: 1-4296-2806-5 (softcover pbk.)
 1. Spiders — Juvenile literature. I. Title. II. Series.
QL458.4.P47 2009
595.4'4 — dc22   2008001458

Summary: A basic field guide format introduces 13 spiders.

About Spiders

Scientists have identified at least 40,000 species of spiders. Scientists group spiders together based on common characteristics. The spiders in this book represent the web-weaving, fishing, jumping, hunting, sac spinning, and ambush types of spiders.

Note to Parents and Teachers

The Pebble First Guides set supports science standards related to life science. In a reference format, this book describes and illustrates 13 spider species. This book introduces early readers to subject-specific vocabulary words, which are defined in the Glossary section. Early readers may need assistance to read some words and to use the Table of Contents, Glossary, Read More, Internet Sites, and Index sections of the book.

Table of Contents

black and yellow garden spider with prey

Length: Male: ¼ to ⅜ inch (6 to 9 millimeters)
Female: ¾ to 1 ⅛ inch (19 to 28 millimeters)

Eats: small flying insects

Lives: gardens

Range: North and South America

Facts:
- web has a zigzag shape in center
- builds webs up to 2 feet (.6 meter) wide

Black Widow Spider

Length: Male: 1 ⅛ inches (29 millimeters)
Female: 1 ½ inches (38 millimeters)

Eats: insects

Lives: woodpiles, barns, garages, hollow logs

Range: United States

Facts:
- female sometimes eats male after mating
- venom is deadly to prey

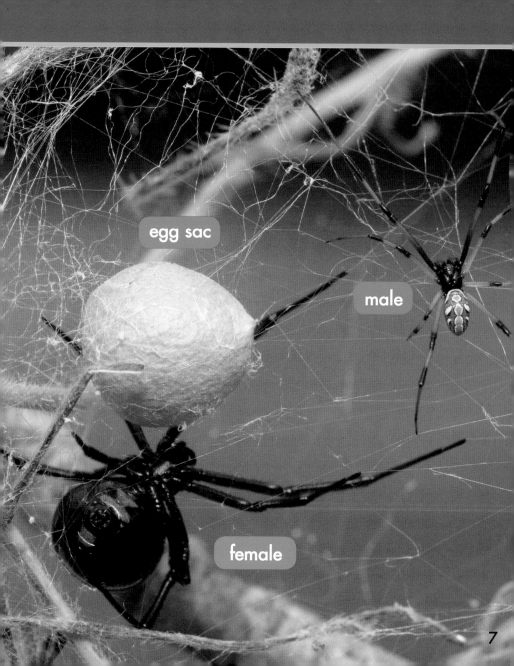

egg sac

male

female

Blonde Tarantula

Length: 3 to 4 inches (70 to 100 millimeters)

Eats: lizards, crickets, beetles, grasshoppers

Lives: burrows dug in desert soil

Range: southwestern United States

Facts: • female lays up to 1,000 eggs
           • female lives up to 20 years

violin mark

Length: Male: ¼ inch (6 millimeters)
Female: ⅜ inch (9.5 millimeters)

Eats: insects

Lives: dark places, such as closets, under rocks

Range: United States

Facts: • called "violin spider" because of mark on body

• has venomous bite

11

Length: Male: ¾ to 1 inch (18 to 24 millimeters)
Female: 1 ⅛ to 1 ¼ inch (28 to 33 millimeters)

Eats: insects, millipedes, other spiders

Lives: burrow with a trapdoor covering

Range: southern California

Facts:
- surprises prey by popping out of trapdoor
- lines burrow with silk

13

Common Sac Spider

Length: ⅛ to ⅜ inch (3 to 10 millimeters)

Eats: small insects

Lives: leaves, bark, under stones

Range: North and South America, Europe, Asia, Africa

Facts:
- tricks enemies because it looks like an ant
- spins a sac to hide in

Length: Male: ⅛ inch (3 millimeters)
Female: ¼ to ⅜ inch (6 to 9 millimeters)

Eats: bees, wasps, butterflies, moths

Lives: flowers, meadows, fields

Range: North America, Europe

Facts: • changes color to blend in with flower
• can walk sideways and backward

Huntsman Spider

Length: Male: ¾ inch (19 millimeters)
Female: 1 inch (24 millimeters)

Eats: cockroaches and other insects

Lives: houses, barns, sheds, bark, woods, gardens

Range: tropical areas throughout world

Facts:
- female carries egg sac under her body
- hunts at night

female and
egg sac

19

Length: Male: ⅜ to ½ inch (9 to 13 millimeters)
Female: ⅝ to ¾ inch (17 to 19 millimeters)

Eats: small insects, tadpoles, small fish

Lives: streams, ponds

Range: North and South America

Facts:
- stays safe by going underwater
- rests legs in water to feel for prey

Spitting Spider

spitting spider
with prey

Length: Male: ⅛ to ¼ inch (3 to 6 millimeters)
Female: ⅜ to ¾ inch (9 to 19 millimeters)

Eats: small insects

Lives: woods, fields, trash, closets

Range: eastern United States

Facts: • spits gumlike substance to catch prey
• female carries egg sac until
spiderlings hatch

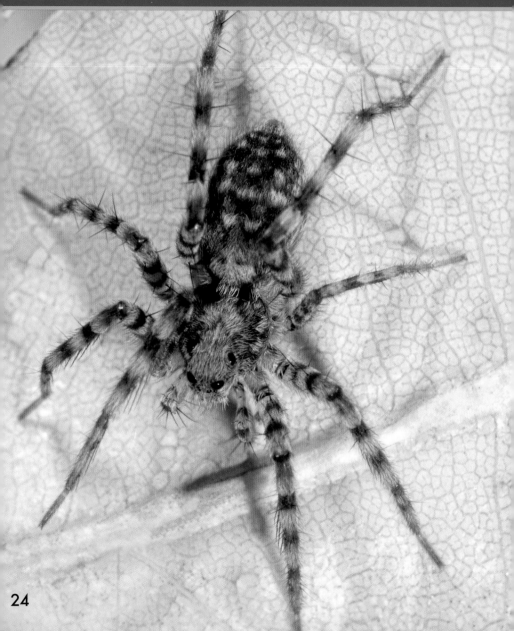

spiderlings

Length: Male: ⅛ to ⅜ inch (3 to 9 millimeters)
Female: ¼ to ⅜ inch (6 to 9 millimeters)

Eats: insects

Lives: soil in grassy fields

Range: North America, Europe

Facts:
- hunts during day
- spiderlings live on female's back for a week after hatching

western lynx spider
with prey

Length: Male: ⅜ to ⅖ inch (9 to 10 millimeters)
Female: ⅜ to ½ inch (9 to 13 millimeters)

Eats: small insects

Lives: grass, shrubs

Range: United States, Mexico

Facts:
- spines on legs used to catch prey
- has long, pointy abdomen

Zebra Jumping Spider

Length: Male: ⅕ to ¼ inch (4 to 6 millimeters)
Female: ⅕ to ³⁄₁₀ inch (4 to 7 millimeters)

Eats: houseflies, beetles, stinkbugs, armyworms

Lives: sunny house walls, window frames,
tree trunks

Range: Europe, North America, northern Asia

Facts: • doesn't build a web
• jumps on prey

zebra jumping spider
with prey

Glossary

abdomen — the end part of a spider's body

burrow — a tunnel or hole in the ground made or used by an animal

hatch — to break out of an egg

insect — a small animal with a hard outer shell, six legs, three body sections, and two antennas; most insects have wings.

mate — to produce young

prey — an animal hunted by another animal for food

sac — something shaped like a bag; some female spiders make sacs to hold their eggs.

venom — poisonous liquid made by some spiders

Read More

Gordon, Sharon. *Guess Who Spins*. Bookworms. Guess Who? New York: Benchmark Books, 2005.

Huggins-Cooper, Lynn. *Minibeasts*. First-Hand Science. North Mankato, Minn.: Smart Apple Media, 2005.

Internet Sites

FactHound offers a safe, fun way to find Internet sites related to this book. All of the sites on FactHound have been researched by our staff.

Here's how:

1. Visit *www.facthound.com*
2. Choose your grade level.
3. Type in this book ID **1429617128** for age-appropriate sites. You may also browse subjects by clicking on letters, or by clicking on pictures and words.
4. Click on the **Fetch It** button.

FactHound will fetch the best sites for you!

Index

Grade: 1
Early-Intervention Level: 25

Editorial Credits
Erika L. Shores, editor; Alison Thiele, designer; Jo Miller, photo researcher

Photo Credits
Alamy/blickwinkel, 28; Graphic Science, 18; Holt Studios International Ltd/
    Nigel Cattlin, 16
Bruce Coleman Inc., 12; Edward L. Snow, 9, 17; Wardene Weisser, 13
Bud Hensley, 26
Edward Trammel, 27
Getty Images Inc./Visuals Unlimited/Rob and Ann Simpson, 10
iStockphoto/sdewdney, cover (wolf spider)
Nature Picture Library/Barry Mansell, 23
Pete Carmichael, 4, 6, 11, 19, 20, 22, 24, 29
Peter Arnold/H. Gehlken, 25
Shutterstock/Christina Richards, cover (black and yellow garden spider);
    Snowleopard1, cover (black widow), 7
SuperStock Inc./age footstock, cover (fishing spider), 21
Tom Murray, 15
Troy Bartlett, 14
UNICORN Stock Photos/Doug Adams, 5
Visuals Unlimited/Gerold and Cynthia Merker, 8